DATE DUE

BASEBALL LEGENDS

Hank Aaron

Grover Cleveland Alexander

Ernie Banks

Albert Belle

Johnny Bench

Yogi Berra

Barry Bonds

Roy Campanella

Roger Clemens

Roberto Clemente

Ty Cobb

Dizzy Dean

Joe DiMaggio

Bob Feller

Lou Gehrig

Bob Gibson

Ken Griffey, Jr.

Rogers Hornsby

Randy Johnson

Walter Johnson

Chipper Jones

Sandy Koufax

Life in the Minor Leagues

Greg Maddux

Mickey Mantle

Christy Mathewson

Willie Mays

Mark McGwire

Stan Musial

Mike Piazza

Cal Ripken, Jr.

Brooks Robinson

Frank Robinson

Jackie Robinson

Pete Rose

Babe Ruth

Nolan Ryan

Mike Schmidt

Tom Seaver

Duke Snider

Warren Spahn

Casey Stengel

Frank Thomas

Honus Wagner

Larry Walker

Ted Williams

Carl Yastrzemski

Cy Young

CHELSEA HOUSE PUBLISHERS

1947—Official Score Card—1947

Cambridge Dodgers

Score Card 5¢

Dodger Park, Cambridge, Md.

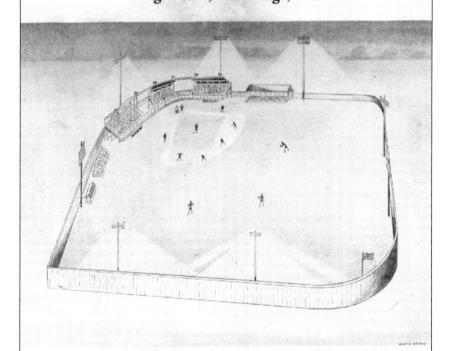

Charles E. Brohawn & Bros., Contractors

BASEBALL LEGENDS

LIFE IN THE MINOR LEAGUES

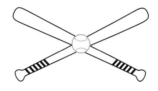

Dennis R. Tuttle

Senior Consultant
Earl Weaver

CHELSEA HOUSE PUBLISHERS
Philadelphia

Produced by Choptank Syndicate, Inc.

Editor and Picture Researcher: Norman L. Macht
Production Coordinator and Editorial Assistant: Mary E. Hull
Design and Production: Lisa Hochstein

CHELSEA HOUSE PUBLISHERS

Editor in Chief: Stephen Reginald
Managing Editor: James Gallagher
Production Manager: Pamela Loos
Art Director: Sara Davis
Director of Photography: Judy L. Hasday
Senior Production Editor: Lisa Chippendale
Publishing Coordinator: James McAvoy
Cover Design and Digital Illustration: Keith Trego

Cover Photos: © David Durochik

The Chelsea House World Wide Web site
address is http://www.chelseahouse.com

First Printing

1 3 5 7 9 8 6 4 2

Library of Congress Cataloging-in-Publication Data

Tuttle, Dennis R.
     Life in the minor leagues / Dennis R. Tuttle; senior consultant, Earl Weaver.
          64 p.   cm.— (Baseball legends)
     Includes bibliographical references (p. 62) and index.
     Summary: Surveys the history of minor league baseball, describing the lives
of players, coaches, umpires, and others involved and discussing developments
in this facet of America's favorite pastime.
     ISBN 0-7910-5160-9
     1. Minor league baseball—United States—History—Juvenile literature.
[1. Minor league baseball—History. 2. Baseball—History.] I. Title. II. Series.
GV863.A1T88 1999
796.357'63'0973— dc21   99-11980
                                                                              CIP

CONTENTS

BASEBALL AT ITS PUREST

"I had a tremendous amount of fun. But the thing you have to remember is: there's a lot of people trying to get your job."
—*Seattle shortstop Alex Rodriguez*

Fans at minor league games enjoy a close-up view of the action. At the ballpark in Lanett, Alabama, of the old Class D Georgia-Alabama League, a special section was reserved for the most vocal of the "bleacher experts" to render instant verdicts on the players' perfor-mance.

For more than 100 years, the minor leagues have been baseball's breeding ground, the true roots of the "national pastime." Almost every major-league star—from Babe Ruth to Mark McGwire—began his professional career in the minors, riding a bus and carrying his own bags in places such as Hickory, North Carolina, Davenport, Iowa, and Butte, Montana.

The players suit up for teams with nicknames such as the Crawdads, River Bandits, and Copper Kings. And while the players' obvious goal is to one day reach the big leagues, the games are a family event with picnics, mascots, and lots of prizes for the fans. A ticket costs only a couple of dollars and the ballparks are so small that foul balls can often be found in the front seat of a parked car, having crashed through the windshield.

For the towns and fans, these are their own Yankees, Red Sox, Cubs, or Dodgers. The teams and players become a staple of the community and a center of activity. There might be a parade through town on opening day, cow-milking contests, or greased pig chases on the field during the season. It's not unusual to see groups of Little Leaguers getting tips from the pros. And some players even get married at home plate before a game, inviting the whole town to attend.

The players and fans get so close in the minors that a family sometimes takes a player into their home for the season. Imagine sitting on your front porch, drinking lemonade with a minor leaguer who may one day become a Hall of Famer.

Teammates and fans in Bluefield, West Virginia, can say they were the first to see the potential of Cal Ripken Jr. in 1978. A kid in Amarillo, Texas, can brag that he once got batting tips from perennial batting champion Tony Gwynn. A collector in Winter Haven, Florida, can show

In Durham, North Carolina, the aroma of curing tobacco covered the field, which was surrounded by cigarette factories.

off an autographed ball that strikeout artist Roger Clemens signed for him long before Clemens became one of the greatest pitchers of all time.

"The thing about the minors," said Seattle Mariners All-Star center fielder Ken Griffey Jr., "is that everybody is from different parts of the world. You have Americans, Dominicans, Puerto Ricans, Canadians, Australians, blacks, whites—kids from poor backgrounds and rich backgrounds, all walks of life. We were all there for the same reason and we were all very young, and we learned a lot about each other. It wasn't as much about winning and losing, but maturing as a player and a person."

The minors offer baseball in its purest and most innocent form. Games are played by eager, inexperienced young men who make dumb mistakes on the field. Many are sent home a failure by the end of their first season. In fact, just one of every 14 minor leaguers will reach the big leagues. But they always believe, even if the belief is impossible. They share such a love for the game that a simple rain delay usually brings players from the dugouts to help the grounds crew cover the infield. Sometimes a player might be recruited to drive the team bus or tape a teammate's ankle.

Bob Hamelin, the 1994 American League Rookie of the Year with the Kansas City Royals recalled, "We had just finished a late game in Greenville, South Carolina. We had about an 11-hour bus trip back to Memphis, so we needed to stop and get something to eat. But everything was closed down. We finally found a Subway that was open. There was one guy working in there, but it was midnight and he was about to close. The whole team busts in there and just sends

MINOR LEAGUE MOMENTS

Hot Potato

In a game on August 31, 1987, Dave Bresnahan, a reserve catcher for Williamsport of the Eastern League, substituted a peeled potato for a baseball and then hurled the potato into left field in an apparent pickoff attempt. The runner on third raced home, but was tagged out by Bresnahan with the real baseball. The umpire called the runner safe and the next day Bresnahan was released.

the poor guy into a panic. So I jump behind the counter and start fixing sandwiches. I got the team fed and on its way."

In 1948, Ray "Little Buffalo" Perry led the Far West League by batting .411 for Redding, California. When he wasn't playing, he served as the team president, general manager, bus driver, trainer, and league vice president. Those extra duties didn't hurt his hitting; he batted .404 in 1949, but lost the batting title by two points.

The lifestyle and playing conditions in the minors are the complete opposite of anything major leaguers experience—from all-night trips on rickety old buses to having just $20 a day for three meals and less than $1,000 a month in salary. Money is often so tight that players get desperate. When former National League All-Star

Ken Griffey Jr. didn't spend much time in the minor leagues, but coming in contact with players from all walks of life helped him grow as a person.

Little Leaguers get many opportunities to learn from the pros at minor league parks. Here Mike Wade of the Frederick Keys demonstrates throwing from the outfield.

Chris Sabo was in the minors, he worked at a fast food restaurant early in the day and then went to the park.

"I remember one time I had to sell my boots to get some food," said Joe Carter, whose home run against the Philadelphia Phillies in the bottom of the ninth inning in Game 6 of the 1993 World Series lifted the Toronto Blue Jays to the world championship. "Can you imagine? Those were $200 boots and I sold them for 40 bucks just so we could eat. That's the way it is in the minor leagues. People talk about being overpaid. Baloney. In the minors, everyone is broke."

"The minor leagues is like bad medicine," said New York Yankees pitcher David Cone. "It didn't taste good going down, but it sure made you feel good later when you thought about it."

Despite the hardships, many players, coaches, and managers later looked back on their minor league days as the most fun they ever had in the game.

KNOXVILLE
Smokies
1958

Where
the STARS
of
TOMORROW
Play
TONIGHT

10¢

2

FROM SURVIVAL TO REVIVAL

"[The best thing about the
minors was] getting out of there."
—*broadcaster Bob Uecker*

A big theme of the minor leagues has always been the opportunity to watch future Hall of Famers at the start of their careers. Although some young players are tagged as "can't miss" prospects, nobody really knows who will make it and who will not.

The minors are often called the bush leagues because in the early days most teams were located in towns far from metropolitan areas, in "the bushes" or "boondocks." But the history of the minors almost parallels that of the major leagues. And in the beginning, the play of the minors was often better.

In 1869, the Cincinnati Red Stockings became the first all-professional team. They barnstormed the country, winning all 57 of their games and creating interest in the sport. The Red Stockings disbanded after the 1870 season and the players went to other up-and-coming professional teams. In 1876, the interest in baseball was so high that eight teams formed the first all-professional conference, the National League, with teams in Chicago, St. Louis, Boston, Philadelphia, New York, Cincinnati, Louisville, and Hartford, Connecticut.

The success of the league created a foundation for pro baseball and convinced another group of men that if pro ball could succeed in bigger cities, another league could survive on a lower level in smaller cities.

In 1877, the International Association became the first "minor" league. Candy Cummings, who developed an underhand curveball after skipping a rock across water, pitched for Lynn, Massachusetts, and served as the league president. John W. "Bud" Fowler played three games for Lynn, making him the first professional black player.

By the end of the 1880s, two dozen minor leagues were in operation—some of which are still active. But poor management, unfulfilled schedules, and rowdy play caused many minor leagues to come and go. In many cases the minor leagues were poorly funded and players would jump from team to team.

The major league owners wanted an agreement with the minors—not in pooling or training players as they do today, but to protect their own big-city clubs and control the growth of pro baseball. The minors always rejected such an alliance, fearing the major league owners were trying to steal their players and kill their teams.

By the start of the 20th century, the star players of the minors were no secret to major league managers and scouts. They raided minor league teams, taking future Hall of Famers such as Clark Griffith, Jack Chesbro, and Wee Willie Keeler without paying the minor league teams. In 1901, Ban Johnson, president of the Western League, formed a new major league, the American League, to challenge the National League. The American League then raided the National League and minors for players.

So the presidents of seven minor leagues formed the National Association of Professional

Baseball Leagues to fight the raiding of their players. They added two leagues totalling 72 teams in four classes: A, B, C, and D. A new class AA was added in 1908 so that the powerful Eastern League, Pacific Coast League, and American Association could draft players from lower minor leagues.

Contracts were drawn up to prevent players from jumping between teams. Owners were restricted on how much they could spend on players. Most of all, the minors told the majors that no player could be taken without compensation. Fearing that its talent pool would dry up without an agreement with the minors, the major leagues agreed to pay up to $7,500 to a minor league team for a player. Selling their top players to the major leagues became a way to help minor league owners stay in business.

Fueled by this new revenue and structured system, the minors quickly became a successful business. By the start of World War I, there were 42 leagues and more than 300 teams. But a new

Built in 1909 at a cost of $5,000, the Warren Ballpark in Bisbee, Arizona, may be the oldest ballpark in the country still used for baseball. It was last the home of a minor league team in 1958, and is now used by a Babe Ruth League and high school teams. In this 1917 photo a crowd gathers for a special event.

By the end of the 1950s, the televising of major league games began to cut into minor league attendance. The minors went into a decline that continued for more than 30 years.

and exciting wave of entertainment that included nightclubs, silent movies, vaudeville, and live music shows began to cut into the minors and majors. With many players serving in World War I, the minors shrank to just nine leagues in 1917. Often no more than a few hundred fans showed up. Times got so tough for many teams that fans were asked to return foul balls in exchange for a ticket to another home game.

Thanks to Babe Ruth and his home runs in the 1920s, baseball on the major league level became more popular than before. The richer teams, like the Yankees, could pay top dollar for minor league stars. Poorer teams could not compete. Branch Rickey, general manager of the St. Louis Cardinals, came up with an ingenious idea: the Cardinals would own their minor league teams and stock them with their own players. Thus the modern farm system was born.

Rickey secretly began to buy teams in 1921, and by 1940 the Cardinals owned 33 teams and more than 500 players. The New York Yankees, Brooklyn Dodgers, and others soon did the same. Interest in the minors and their prospects thrived. Many leagues closed during World War II, but a post-war boom produced a record 59 leagues, 448 teams, and 10,000 players in 1949. Attendance reached a record 39.7 million.

But the minors were destined for another recession. American life changed in the 1950s. Beach resorts and other family vacation centers lured away fans. Air-conditioning, once limited to large buildings or theaters, was now available in smaller units for homes. Improvements in roads and cars and air travel allowed people to take trips farther and easier, making vacation resorts popular. And most of all, there was the invention of television.

By the middle of the 1950s, Americans were watching about three hours of TV each day. Fans could watch major league games on TV almost every day, seeing heroes such as Ted Williams, Mickey Mantle, Willie Mays, and Stan Musial rather than just reading about them in the newspapers. Suddenly, there was no need to go to the local ballpark to see baseball. By 1956, 240 teams had gone out of business; minor league attendance dropped to 17 million.

Struggling major league teams began to move into successful minor league markets. The Boston Braves moved to Milwaukee in 1953 and the St. Louis Browns to Baltimore in 1954. The Brooklyn Dodgers, the most successful National

Bet You Didn't Know ...

The first night baseball game played with permanent lights was not at Cincinnati's Crosley Field in 1935, but on May 2, 1930, in Des Moines, Iowa. Teams had been testing night baseball as early as 1909, and the Kansas City Monarchs were using portable systems to light their night games when the Des Moines team erected lights to boost attendance.

League team of the '50s, went to Los Angeles in 1958, with the New York Giants switching to San Francisco the same year.

The transfer of other teams and the expansion of the major leagues swallowed up the biggest minor league cities. In 1962, the minors were reorganized. The top leagues were class AAA with the second tier being AA. Classes C and D were formed into class A, and rookie leagues were created for raw prospects just out of college or high school. The minors would play just 144 games and the rookie leagues 66.

The big league clubs paid most of the players' salaries and controlled the flow of players from one level to the next, thus creating the current "feeder" system of players. In 1966 the major league draft of amateur players began; minor league owners no longer had the burden of signing or paying players. They only had to worry about marketing and operating their teams.

This did not stop the rapid attendance decline. By the mid-1970s, attendance had dwindled to 12 million. But in 1981, the fate of the minors changed. That summer, the major league players went on strike, walking off the field for 51 days.

Major league teams looking to fill the void often broadcast games of their minor league affiliates. Fans rediscovered smaller, homey old parks and the feel of baseball innocence in place of the domed stadiums, artificial turf, expensive concessions, and players who wouldn't sign autographs. Minor league teams that had sold for just $1,000 suddenly became worth millions. In 1983, the Louisville Redbirds of the American Association became the first team to draw a million fans in a season.

The growth continued into the 1990s; by 1998 there were 21 leagues and 237 teams. Attendance

increased in 14 of the 16 years after the 1981 strike. Sales of souvenirs such as T-shirts and caps generated more than $175 million for the minors in the mid-1990s. Ownership gradually shifted back to local investors, who often included actors, singers, and politicians. Traditional minor league cities that had lost teams over the years such as Nashville; Wilmington, Delaware; Ottawa, Ontario; and New Haven, Connecticut, were given new franchises that thrived. In 1993, the Northern League returned after 22 years.

Thanks to modern marketing and promotion, minor league baseball was booming once again.

The Trenton Thunder of the Eastern League play at Mercer County Waterfront Park, a 6,700-seat stadium built on the shores of the Delaware River in 1994. Comfortable, modern ballparks built with old-time touches replaced the rickety old wooden grandstands of the past in many minor league cities in the 1990s.

3

A GRAND TIME AT THE BALLPARK

"You never knew what was going to happen next."
—*Darryl Strawberry in St. Paul*

Calling himself the "Clown Prince of Baseball," the tall, skinny, double-jointed Max Patkin entertained crowds at minor league parks for more than 50 years. A one-time minor league pitcher, he traveled thousands of miles every season, doing his act from the coach's box during the game.

From the earliest days of the minor leagues, owners have used promotions to lure fans to the ballpark and entertain them beyond the game. Free cigars, horse shows, and dancing contests gradually shifted to circus acts and celebrity appearances to mascots, giveaways, and rock concerts. The first and most popular promotion was Ladies Day, where women either got into the game free or at a discount. During World War II, owner Bill Veeck of the then-minor league Milwaukee Brewers took Ladies Day a step further. On Rosie the Riveter Day, if the women who worked in the factories came to the park in their welding gear, ushers wearing tuxedos served them breakfast.

During the last years of the Great Depression, 1936 Olympic 100-meter gold medalist Jesse Owens would come to a minor league park and race a fan, player, or local high school star in a sprint across the field. Owens often gave the competition a 10-yard head start, but with his world record 10.3-second speed, he rarely lost.

A man who called himself Captain Dynamite liked to blow himself out of a box; once in West Palm Beach, Florida, he burned up the pitcher's mound and infield grass. At games in Portland, Maine, when a Sea Dog player hits a home run, a lighthouse rises above the center field fence and sounds a deep whistle, and a bright light spins around the top. In Durham, North Carolina, when a Bulls player hits a homer, a giant mechanical bull sign starts snorting, wagging its tail, blinking his red eyes, and blowing smoke.

Jim Paul, owner of the El Paso Diablos of the Texas League, said, "What we did was make it fun to come to the park. We danced in the aisles. We had a promotion every night and gave away trucks and pizzas and had 10-cent beer nights and brought in the Famous Chicken. We had jugglers and mimes."

When an opposing pitcher was knocked out of the game, the El Paso fans stood up and waved white tissues and sang "Bye-Bye Baby." When an El Paso pitcher was yanked, it became a tradition for the opposing players to come out of the dugout and wave white towels. Everybody loved it, including the players.

Players might sing the national anthem or a famous actor might be a base coach for an inning. Mascots such as the Famous Chicken and the Phillie Phanatic brought huge crowds because they always made people laugh—usually at the umpires' expense.

As owner of the St. Paul Saints of the independent Northern League, Mike Veeck created wacky gimmicks that made fans flock to the park. Veeck once had nuns giving massages and sets

A minor league version of the knothole gang brought kids into the ballpark and helped boost sno-cone sales. Kids also got in free by turning in foul balls hit over the roof into the parking lot.

of twins as ushers. Another time he held a sumo wrestling match. He hired a woman pitcher, Ila Borders.

"You never knew what was going to happen next," said New York Yankees outfielder Darryl Strawberry, who spent time in St. Paul during the 1996 season. "It was a lot of fun for the fans and players. After being in the big leagues for 13 years, you forget about the roots of the game and how far you have come. That month I spent in St. Paul reminded me of what baseball was all about. I really enjoyed the atmosphere around the team and the ballpark there. It was the most fun I've had playing in a long time."

At Midland, Texas, of the Texas League, when a home team player hits a home run, fans take up a collection of money for him by passing around a cap.

Alan Trammell, who played 20 years with the Detroit Tigers, recalled, "In the first game of a doubleheader, when I was with the Montgomery Rebels of the double-A Southern League, some fan gets on the loud speaker and says, 'The first Rebel to hit a home run gets 50 bucks.' No one hit a home run in the first game. In the second game, he gets on the loud speaker again and says, 'The first Rebel to hit a home run gets a hundred bucks.'

"Well, we were getting our butts kicked and I hit a home run, my first professional home run. I round the bases and as soon as I cross the plate, the guy leans over the dugout and hands me a hundred dollar bill."

Perhaps the greatest draw of all was Max Patkin, the "Clown Prince of Baseball." For over 50 years, Patkin traveled to about 150 ballparks each season and did his goofy routine of being

MINOR LEAGUE MOMENTS

Mascot Manager

On June 29, 1989, Mal Fichman, manager of Boise in the Northwest League, was ejected from a game for arguing. He went to the clubhouse, dressed in the Hawks' mascot suit, and returned to the field, where he led fans in cheers and continued to direct his team. He was fined and suspended one game.

a baseball doofus. His body moved like he was made of soft rubber, and he stumbled around mocking players while they warmed up. He wore a uniform with a question mark in place of a number, which was appropriate because you always wondered what he would do next. He drew his biggest laughs when he became a human geyser, blowing water from his mouth six feet straight into the sky.

General managers of small-town teams were kept busy lining up promotions to help boost attendance. Some of the gimmicks of 50 years ago are still used today. Teams often depended on concession sales to make ends meet; they didn't lose any money when they let big eaters in free.

IF YOU WEIGH
200 LBS. OR MORE
YOU WILL BE
ADMITTED FREE
TO THE BALL GAME ON
FAT MAN'S NIGHT
THURSDAY JULY 19
VALLEY VS
LAGRANGE
COME TO GATE 1
TO BE WEIGHED
AND GET A
CHANCE FOR
THE SPECIAL
FAT MAN'S
PRIZE

*The Knoxville Smokies
turned the Tennessee-
Florida football rivalry
into a news-making
promotion in 1998.
When Florida coach
Steve Spurrier bad-
mouthed the Tennessee
Vols, the Smokies invited
fans to try to sail a
paper airplane into
Spurrier's mouth.*

"I was umpiring in the Carolina League in 1967 when me and my partner were late for a doubleheader in Winston-Salem," said the late umpire John McSherry. "They held the game waiting for us. All of this was happening with Max Patkin appearing that night. So we had a decent crowd. My partner was a little agitated about being late, so in about the fourth inning he got rid of the catcher, a guy named Mike Jackson. He threw him out. Then he threw out the Winston-Salem manager, Bill Slack.

"Now we go in between games, come back out, and get ready for our meeting at home plate. Slack is still so mad that he refuses to come out with the lineup card. He says he'll come out when he's good and ready.

Mascots include Donkey-hotey of the Butte, Montana, Copper Kings, shown here wearing a cheesehead on "Green Bay Packers Night."

FUN AT THE BALLPARK

More than any other element, contests and fan giveaways separate the minors from the major leagues. It might be a free car wash for the dirtiest car in the parking lot or a race to first base by fans wearing swimming flippers. Whatever the event, it is designed to keep fans entertained between innings and make them feel special at the ballpark. A look at some of the more popular promotions:

Bingo—A very popular game at minor league stadiums in Florida, where a program has a Bingo board and the announcer calls out numbers between innings.

Dash for Cash—A pile of money is scattered around and the contestant has just a few seconds to grab as much money as he can. Sometimes this game is done by putting money in a phone booth and have it blowing around or putting coins at the bottom of a kiddie pool and having a fan dive for the money.

Dizzy Bat Race—Two or more fans stand near the plate, place their foreheads on the end of a bat that is standing upright and spin around 10 times. Then, they try to race to first base—which in most cases is impossible because the fan is so dizzy he can't do anything but fall down like he's drunk.

Home Run Inning—There are lots of variations on this one, but the most common is during one inning a fan's name is picked out of a barrel for each player who bats for the home team. If a player hits a home run, the fan wins a prize, such as free tickets to another game.

Mascot Race—A fan, usually a kid, races the team mascot around the bases and the mascot always loses—normally by falling down in some funny way.

Racing the mascot around the bases is a between-innings feature at many minor league games. The mascot usually manages to lose every race. The winner sometimes gets a huge box of cereal as big as he or she is.

"So I walk over to the dugout and say, 'Bill, don't bother to come out with the lineup cards 'cause you're gone again.' Then he came out with lineup cards. I said, 'Bill, I can't take those from you because you're not here.' To which he turned around, knocked my partner's hat off, called him every name in the book, called me every name in the book, and we have to call for the cops. There's six cops in the stands and they all turned their backs and went the other way. It took us about 45 minutes to get rid of Slack. And we got rid of that kid Jackson again, too.

"The best part was, Patkin comes out to do his act and he runs past me and says, 'How am I gonna follow you two guys?' "

Bet You Didn't Know ...

Omaha outfielder Glen Gorbous heaved a baseball 445' 10" on August 1, 1957, breaking the record held by Minneapolis's Don Grate.

4

MORE THAN
JUST A GAME

**"I needed six seasons to learn the game,
learn what I was good at and not so good at."**
—*Wade Boggs*

The minor leagues are an advanced school for playing baseball. Once you excel at one level you go up to the next level, and the next, and the next, until you reach the majors—if you make it.

But it's not as simple as passing a test. Just one of every 16,000 who play organized amateur baseball ever make the major leagues. Half of the first-round draft picks—the best of the amateur prospects—never play one game in the majors.

The major leagues' expansion to 30 teams opened more jobs for players; the average salary of $1.3 million a year inspired even more to work harder and keep trying. But for every Barry Bonds, a can't-miss prospect and future Hall of Famer who played less than two seasons in the minors, there are hundreds of players who return home each year a humble failure, having never reached the big leagues. Hall of Fame managers Joe McCarthy, who guided the Yankees to seven pennants in the 1930s and '40s, and Earl Weaver

Fans from Jamestown, New York, to Jacksonville, Florida, watched 6'10" left-hander Randy Johnson struggle to gain control of his fastball for four years before he made his major league debut.

of the Baltimore Orioles never played a day in the majors.

Homesickness and loneliness send more rookies home than injuries. In high school and college, parents and friends were at the games to cheer for them. Suddenly they found themselves far from home, often playing before a huge crowd of sometimes hostile strangers. Many young players never make the adjustment.

Sometimes the necessary work habits aren't there. Cy Young Award winner Roger Clemens said, "In the minor leagues, I passed a lot of kids who definitely had more talent than I did. But they never made it. Some of them couldn't distinguish between the time to play and the time to do their work."

Seattle's star shortstop Alex Rodriguez broke in at Appleton, Wisconsin, in 1994. Minor league fans had little chance to get to know him; two years later he led the American League in hitting with a .358 average.

Sometimes a player just needs to get a lucky break and get traded or released to another team. But others might take longer to bloom. Often compared to Hall of Famer Sandy Koufax (who never spent a day in the minors), Randy Johnson threw fastballs nearly 100 miles per hour and had more strikeouts in the 1990s than any other pitcher. But early in his career, Johnson had terrible control. He was in the Montreal Expos' system for five years and averaged seven walks per nine innings. He also averaged almost 10 strikeouts per nine innings. But his record was just 28–26 with a 4.11 earned run average. It wasn't until three years after Johnson was traded to the Seattle Mariners and he was 30 years old that he mastered control and became a dominant pitcher.

For the most part, a player's progress through the minors comes down to a competition with a teammate or someone in the system who plays the same position. When Cal Ripken was the Baltimore Orioles' shortstop, there was virtually no hope that anyone in their minor league system would ever replace him. The last thing a promising shortstop wanted was to be drafted by the Orioles. Ripken broke Lou Gehrig's record of playing 2,130 consecutive games and, until 1997, when he was moved to third base, had been the team's shortstop for 15 years. When shortstops good enough to play in the majors came up in the Orioles' system, they were either moved to another position or traded.

Time in the minors can be a struggle for even the very best prospects. Juan Gonzalez of the Texas Rangers, the 1996 and '98 American League Most Valuable Player and one of the greatest Latin-American home run hitters, failed

MINOR LEAGUE MOMENTS

Playing the Angles

On July 8, 1955, pitcher Bill Greason of Houston in the Texas League pulled off one of the rarest plays in baseball by getting an unassisted putout at the plate. Greason's pitch sailed over the catcher's head and hit a concrete rail on the grandstand. Then it ricocheted back to the plate, where Greason, charging to cover, caught the rebound and tagged out the runner trying to score from third.

to hit a homer in his 60 games in rookie ball. Fifty-one of his 56 hits were singles. "I had it in my mind I wanted to make the major leagues," he said. "I knew I'd have to go through this. I never let down, although I got discouraged."

"I went to Tampa of the Florida State League when I first signed and I really struggled," said New York Yankees shortstop Derek Jeter, who was 18 years old when he signed out of high school. "You think it's going to be like high school and you walk in and play just like you did. But the thing about high school is: if you're successful and you've never struggled before, you've never had to cope with the failure. Now, all of a sudden, you're playing with and against the best people in baseball. Our first games were a double-header against the White Sox team in Sarasota. I was 0-for-8. I made three errors with seven strikeouts. I was thinking, 'Man, I should have gone to college.'"

What many fans don't see or understand is how hard the players have to work. "When you get into pro ball, you play every day. It's your job. It's not school work," added first baseman Will Clark.

Baseball on the professional level is a huge adjustment—personally and professionally. Playing every day is a lot harder than two or three games a week. A big high school star suddenly finds himself surrounded by all-staters or All-American competition.

While the game is fun, it is very demanding. Players in the minors arrive at the ballpark about three to four hours before a game for special coaching, extra batting practice, and individual workout sessions.

Oakland second baseman Scott Spiezio had spent his entire amateur and pro career on the

left side of the infield. But when the A's asked him to switch to second base, he and infield coach Ron Washington worked for about 90 minutes every day, fielding nearly 200 balls, and working on footwork, throws to the shortstop, touching second base on relay throws—the works. Spiezio worked so hard that his hands were blue from taking ground balls. Then he had to play in a game.

"It's a pretty big difference from playing third," he said. "It's not just about being on a different side of the infield, but a different angle on the ball. And there's a lot more ground to cover. A lot of things come into play, too, like making that

Jackie Robinson became the first black major league player in the 20th century with the Brooklyn Dodgers in 1947. But he played a year in the minor leagues first, enduring racial harassment on and off the field. Here he crosses the plate after hitting a home run for the Montreal Royals of the International League.

In his four years in the minors, former number one pick Chipper Jones of Atlanta was rated among the top major league prospects at every level where he played. Here he takes a throw at second base for Richmond of the International League.

first step toward the ball, getting an angle, and seeing the ball come off the bat."

Even with so much practice and coaching, minor league players still make a lot of mistakes. As a result, strange things happen on the field. One time a pitcher for Toledo didn't see manager Pat Corrales call for an appeal play at second base. With the runner on third, the second baseman standing on second, and the shortstop backing him up, the pitcher threw the ball home. The batter, realizing the fielders were out of position, bunted the ball. "Of course, there wasn't anybody to field the ball because all of our middle infielders were at second base," Corrales recalled. "The run scored and the guy who bunted the ball got a double."

But for the exceptional prospects, there's little patience for such mistakes. They're expected to learn quickly or suffer the worst fate a minor leaguer can experience: being released or demoted. Most of the players in rookie leagues will have to deal with the crushing blow of being handed their release.

"In my second year in pro ball, at Class A Lynchburg in 1983, I was 0–3 and really struggling," said 1985 Cy Young Award winner Doc Gooden. "They were about to send me back down to Kingsport or Little Falls. It was right in the middle of a game and John Cumberland was our pitching coach. He came out to the pitcher's mound.

"'You're a lot better than this. You're pitching like you're scared,' Cumberland said. 'I don't know what's wrong with you, but if you don't get it turned around right here, I'm gonna get them to send you out of here!'

"Well, I got it turned around right then and there," Gooden said. "I finished the year 19–4, and the next year I was up with the Mets. I think that visit to the mound by John Cumberland sticks out more than anything that ever happened to me."

When Cal Ripken Jr., broke in at Bluefield, West Virginia, in 1978, he was not an instant success. He made a lot of errors, and the stands were so close to the field he could not avoid hearing the few hundred fans yelling at him, "Go back to Little League." But he later said his rookie year "was the most fun I ever had in baseball because we were all the same. As you go up and up, it gets to be more of a job."

5

THE WORST JOB ON EARTH

"The managers are always going to test you."
—*Former major league umpire Steve Palermo*

Pam Postema tried to become the first woman umpire in the major leagues, but she gave up after 13 years in the minors, starting in 1977. She once ejected a batboy for refusing to retrieve a chair thrown on the field by a manager. Here she makes a call in an American Association game in 1987.

The most abused people at baseball games are the umpires. They get booed, second-guessed, cursed at, and sometimes physically attacked.

Like the players, umpires in the minors are getting on-the-job training. They make mistakes. "In many cases you know the rules better than the umpires," said long-time coach Harry Dunlop. "Sometimes even the fans know better." An umpire's job is made harder because the minor league parks are small and the fans are close to the field. Small towns may not have enough police officers to provide security against angry fans. Dressing rooms are usually underneath the stands, where the fans can easily get to them. When former major league umpire Steve Palermo was in the Carolina League, fans started kicking in the door to the umpires' locker room after a game in Rocky Mount, North Carolina.

"We had to fight them off. They smashed in the top half of the door," he said. "We tossed a mask at them from our side of the door, and fists and bottles were being thrown from their side out in the hallway. The police were a little reluctant to help us at first because they thought it might turn into some sort of lynching. They let it build up and it got real hairy, then they followed us out of town."

There was once a former big league pitcher named Jim Bluejacket who turned to umpiring. He lasted three games—the last of which saw him being chased over the center field fence by an angry mob of players and fans.

Except for the constant berating and abuse, the umpires' lives are similar to the players'. They get paid about as much and their travel can be worse. "This will tell you how bad the money was," said National League umpire Ed Montague of his days in the California League. "I also sold beer at Oakland Raiders games and I made more money selling beer in one night than I made in two weeks working as an umpire."

Rookie league umpires earning $600 a month have about $10 a day to live on after taxes and expenses. Traveling together in pairs, they might have enough money to stay in a rundown rooming house or third-rate motel, often in a room with only one bed. They would take turns sleeping on the floor. In small towns they relied on fast-food places to eat, or they might go into a store and buy a loaf of bread and some baloney to make sandwiches.

"It ain't called the *minor* leagues for nothing," said former umpire Dave Pallone.

In the lower levels of the minors the umpires drive from city to city. Having a smashed windshield, slashed tires, and a mob of angry fans chasing you out of town is a tough way to make

MINOR LEAGUE MOMENTS

Gulls in the Outfield

On August 12, 1952, a game at Beaumont, Texas, was interrupted by a flock of seagulls. The gulls tormented the players for several minutes before settling in center field to watch the game.

a living. "Several times in the Ohio State League and the Carolina State League, the ballplayers had to help us off the field," said former umpire Bill McKinley. "They would form a line with bats in their hands and we would walk through it, get in our cars, and leave."

In most minor leagues there are just two umpires—one behind the plate and one calling the bases. There are 103 pages of rules for an umpire to learn. There is no way the umps can be on top of every play.

"I always tried to treat the umpires with a lot of respect. They have an awful tough job to do, and in the minors they're training, too," said Cleveland Indians coach Johnny Goryl, who spent 12 years managing in the minors. "But we had one guy in the Midwest League; seemed every time he made a call it was against us. We were playing in Davenport, Iowa, and he was having a tough day calling the bases. In the two-man system he had to be on the grass part of the infield behind second so he could make calls at first, second or third. He just happened to be in the wrong place at the wrong time and some guy hit a line drive that went off his head. I hollered out of the dugout, 'I hope that knocked some sense into you!' With that response, he ejected me."

It's not unusual to hear of fans, scoreboard operators, announcers, and even team mascots getting thrown out of a game. In 1995, the public address announcer of the Abilene Prairie Dogs of the Texas-Louisiana League was tossed after Abilene manager Charlie Kerfeld capped an argument by shaking his eyeglasses at home plate umpire Mel Chettum. The announcer was asked by the team's media director, Bruce Unrue, to kill time during the argument by reading

Davy Cricket, mascot of the Lubbock Crickets in the Texas-Louisiana League, claimed he was just standing there minding his own business during a players' brawl, but the umpire threw him out of the game.

*One umpire who became
a favorite of fans was
Harry "Steamboat"
Johnson, who worked
37 years in the minor
leagues—28 of them in
the Southern Association.
In 1949, New Orleans
fans honored him with
a special night. He joined
in the fun by wearing
dark glasses and using
a "seeing-eye dog" while
two policemen escorted
him to the plate, where
he received numerous gifts.*

the next promotion over the loudspeaker. As it turned out, the announcement was for a local eyeglass maker.

"It was totally innocent, but the umps didn't think it was funny," Unrue said. "Of course, the crowd thought that was hilarious."

Two weeks later, the Prairie Dogs were involved in another incident with the same umpire. After a beanball fight broke out in a game against the Lubbock Crickets, the umpires tossed the managers, a handful of players, the scoreboard operators, and the Lubbock mascot, Davy

Cricket. "I was just standing there by the third base line, and [the umpire] pushed me from behind," the mascot said. "He shoves me and says, 'Get this bug off the field.' "

Today's umpires actually have it better than the umpires of yesteryear. In the early days of minor league ball, the umpires were so abused that leagues could barely recruit enough to have one ump at a game. It was especially bad in the Western Association located among small towns in Oklahoma. In 1921, 17 umpires quit before the season was half over. Umpires were mugged, shot at, and even threatened with being hanged from a tree. Former major league umpire Joe Rue, who called his first professional game in the Western Association that year, said that fans were so bad in one city they wouldn't let him under the grandstands during a rain delay. While he stood in the pouring rain, fans threw mud-balls at him.

At almost any time a play can unfold that the umpire has never seen. This happens often in the minors, where the players not only make more mistakes than major leaguers, but the smaller ballparks can lead to bizarre plays and leave rules open to interpretation. For example, every now and then in the Florida State League, a batted ball will hit a flying seagull, or a pelican will drop a fish on the field in the middle of a play. One day in 1962 in Crowley, Louisiana, the umpires had to use bats to kill a poisonous snake that had crawled onto the outfield from a nearby swamp. A Texas League game at Midland was once postponed due to a grasshopper invasion. In 1951, a Pony League game between Olean and Batavia was disrupted by a skunk that wouldn't be chased away by either

Bet You Didn't Know ...

In 1902, Corsicana of the Texas League beat Texarkana 51–3 for the most lopsided win in the history of baseball. Corsicana hit 21 homers and had 53 hits—all against starting pitcher Bill DeWitt. Corsicana's Nig Clarke slugged eight homers in eight at-bats. Corsicana won a record 27 consecutive games that season.

*Steamboat Johnson
rubs up the baseballs
with a special dirt in the
umpires' dressing room in
Birmingham's Rickwood
Field. In his 28 years in
the Southern Association,
Johnson said he was
proud of the fact that he
had been "pop-bottled
twice in every ballpark
in the league."*

the players or umpires. The contest, after a long delay, was completed before virtually empty stands.

"I was at double-A Bristol in 1978 and we were playing a night game against the A's team in Jersey City," said six-time American League batting champion Wade Boggs. "I forgot who hit the ball, but he hit a popup to the infield. I started running behind the mound to catch the ball. I glanced down to see the other infielders converging on the ball and looked back up to pick up the ball. But the second I took my eye off the ball to see the other infielders, I never saw the ball again. It never came down!

"We had all converged on the ball. It wasn't hit high enough to be blown out of the park or to the outfield. No one could find the ball. None of the players. None of the umpires. No one. People in the stands said it didn't come down in the stands. People were asking everybody, 'Did you see the ball?'

"We looked around the infield to see if it had plunked in the grass. We searched the perimeter of the outfield. We were all standing around looking at each other, waiting for it to hit. But it never did. It just never came down.

"So they gave the batter a ground-rule double. They couldn't figure out what happened to the ball. And no one knows to this day what happened to it."

6

HEROES OF THE BUSH LEAGUES

"I told him that the only thing I cared about was that I had to pretty much treat him like everyone else."

—Terry Francona, who managed Michael Jordan in the minors

When Michael Jordan switched from the basketball court to the baseball diamond in 1994, he discovered that it was harder to hit a curve than a three-pointer. Playing for the AA Birmingham Barons, he ducks away from an inside pitch before flying out in his first professional at-bat against the Chattanooga Lookouts.

Barry Bonds, Alex Rodriguez, Ken Griffey Jr., Tony Gwynn, and Nomar Garciaparra are major league superstars who were so good that they spent very little time in the minors. But most fans have never heard of Spencer Harris, Ike Boone, Joe Hauser, Hector Espino, Joe Bauman, Bill Thomas, or Tony Freitas, who rode more buses, stayed in more cheap hotels, and played on more bad fields than just about anyone. They spent almost their entire careers in the minor leagues, where they not only became superstars of the bushes, but set records that are mind-boggling even today.

Harris played 27 seasons and is the minors' all-time leader in runs, doubles, total bases, and hits with 3,617. Boone batted .370 over his 17-year career, the best in the history of organized baseball. Hauser, a slugging first baseman, is the only player to hit 60 or more homers twice (63 in 1930 and 69 in 1933). Espino felt so loyal to his native Mexico that he refused many offers from the big leagues and played 24 years in the Mexican League. He retired in 1984 as the minors' all-time leader with 484 home runs.

Bill Thomas pitched 26 seasons and won 383 games. Tony Freitas won 342, including 20 or more nine times. In 1948, Bob Crues hit 69 homers for Amarillo of the Class C West Texas–New Mexico League to tie Hauser's record. Crues also drove in an incredible 254 runs and batted .404, which wasn't too bad for a fellow who broke in as a pitcher before an arm injury forced him to switch to the outfield.

It seems strange that players with such lofty numbers spent so much time in the minors. Before the 1960s, when major league clubs started controlling the players in the minors and the current player development system began, players routinely hung around the bush leagues for 10, 15, even 20 years. It was not unusual for major leaguers whose skills had declined to go back to the minors. Nor was it unusual for a player who simply loved to play baseball to keep it as his summer job.

Some minor league players became famous in other fields. Randall Poffo played four seasons, hitting just .254. The only mark he left on pro baseball was that he seemed to stay out too late and his oversleeping always angered his managers. He is known today as Randy "Macho Man" Savage, the world champion pro wrestler.

"I was playing at Tampa for the Reds in 1974, and Macho Man Savage was on our team," said former teammate Joel Youngblood, a major league coach. "One day we were taking batting practice

MINOR LEAGUE MOMENTS

45 Complete Games

On September 15, 1906, Glen Leibhardt of Memphis defeated Montgomery on the final day of the season for his 35th victory and 45th complete game of the season. At one point he completed a record 40 games in a row.

Baseball's all-time single-season home run king never played a day in the big leagues. First baseman Joe Bauman hit 72 home runs for the Roswell Rockets of the Longhorn League in 1954. Here he is greeted by Rockets third baseman Stubby Greer, who was also a co-owner of the team.

72 HOMERS: BAUMAN'S AMAZING SEASON

In 1954, Joe Bauman, a 32-year-old first baseman for Roswell, New Mexico, tore up the Longhorn League by hitting .400 with 224 RBI and a .916 slugging percentage. Just days before the end of the season, it appeared he didn't have enough time to break the home run record of 69, held by Joe Hauser and Bob Crues. But Bauman hit four homers and drove in 10 runs in a game against Sweetwater.

"It went from an impossibility to a possibility in one night," he said.

Bauman tied the record with three days left. Then, in Roswell's doubleheader to close the season at Artesia, Bauman homered three times, hitting number 70 in the first game and 71 and 72 in the second.

"It was the ultimate thrill, as far as I was concerned," Bauman said.

Bauman played just two more seasons and finished a nine-year minor league career with 337 homers. But he never played a game in the big leagues. In fact, he played only one game above Class A ball.

"Back in those days," he said, "ballplayers didn't make much money. In 1954, I made $500 or $600 a month and that was as much or more than some guys in the big leagues. I owned a gas station and when the season was over I had to take care of business. That's the way things were back then. Now, yes, I do believe I would have gotten a better shot at the big leagues—even if it was just for one season."

Bet You Didn't Know ...

The fly swatter was invented on the inspiration of a Western League game between Topeka and Wichita in 1911. Dr. Samuel Crumbine, head of the Kansas state Board of Health, was working to reduce the number of flies, which carried typhoid fever. He took a break to attend a baseball game, where he heard fans cry "swat the fly" for a sacrifice fly with a runner on third. Dr. Crumbine left the game and started a public health campaign called "Swat the Fly." When teacher and scoutmaster Frank Rose heard about it, he organized his troop to make yardsticks with wire mesh attached to the end. They called it a fly bat, but Dr. Crumbine suggested calling it a fly swatter.

and he's running late. Russ Nixon was our manager and he'd had enough of Randy being late all the time. Russ was standing at the gate there on the field, looking at his watch. When the time came, Russ closed and locked the gate. All of a sudden, you heard somebody yelling and come running up there full tilt to hit that gate. It was Randy. He had gotten a running start and jumped up on the gate and was just hanging there. Then he started climbing and he kind of just flipped himself over the top and came into practice like nothing was wrong. That was the funniest thing."

When Michael Jordan left the three-time defending champion Chicago Bulls and signed with the Chicago White Sox in 1994, the minors had never had such a famous rookie. Jordan was 32 at the time and had won the NBA scoring title six years in a row. He was the most famous athlete in the world, yet there he was playing in the bushes with the Birmingham Barons of the Class AA Southern League.

Huge crowds showed up wherever the Barons played. But Jordan didn't ask for, or receive, any special treatment. He was making over $50 million a year from his endorsements, but he still rode the team bus and stayed in the same hotels with his teammates. He came to practice early and stayed late after games to work. However, at 6' 6", he had a huge strike zone and too many holes in his swing. He batted just over .200 and by the end of the 1995 basketball season, he was back with the Bulls.

Pro football Hall of Famers Jim Thorpe, Don Hutson, and Sammy Baugh played minor league baseball. Thorpe won two gold medals in the 1912 Olympics, but had to return them when it

GREAT FEATS
OF THE MINORS

Because there are so many leagues and many more games, some incredible records have taken place in the minors. A look at the top nine all-time greatest feats in minor league history:

1 On May 13, 1952, Ron Neccai of Bristol in the Appalachian League hurled a no-hitter against Welch, West Virginia, in which he struck out 27 batters. One batter was retired on a groundout. But because his catcher missed a third strike and allowed the runner to reach first base, Neccai fanned four in an inning.

2 Joe DiMaggio, an 18-year-old outfielder with San Francisco of the Pacific Coast League, hit in a record 61 consecutive games during the 1933 season.

3 Pitching for the Winchester, Kentucky, Hustlers against the Lexington Colts in 1909, Fred Toney pitched 17 innings of no-hit ball and finally won the game when his team pushed across a run on a squeeze play in the bottom of the 17th.

4 The Muskogee, Oklahoma, team of the Southwestern League lost 38 consecutive games in 1923—the longest losing streak in the history of organized baseball.

5 In 1954, Joe Bauman of the Roswell, New Mexico, Rockets hit 72 home runs in the class C Longhorn League, breaking the mark of 69 homers by Joe Hauser with Minneapolis in 1933 and Bob Crues of Amarillo in 1948.

Ron Neccai

6 Spencer Harris served 27 years in the minors (and just four in the majors) and retired in 1948 as the minors' career leader in runs, doubles, total bases, walks, and hits with 3,617.

7 On June 5, 1914, pitcher John Cantley of Opelika of the Georgia–Alabama League hit three grand slams and a single for 15 runs batted in to lead his team to a 19-1 victory against Talledega.

8 Stan Wasiak spent 37 years managing in the minors, winning a record 2,530 games. He never managed in the majors.

9 Vince Coleman of Macon in the South Atlantic League stole 145 bases in 1983, breaking the record of 124 set by James Johnston of San Francisco in 1913. But Coleman barely won the stolen base title; Donell Nixon of Bakersfield in the California League had 144 steals.

was learned that he had played in the minors for $60 a month in 1910. Hutson, who played for the Green Bay Packers and was football's first great receiver, playing batted over .300 during his two minor league seasons. Quarterback Slingin' Sammy Baugh went from leading the Washington Redskins to the NFL championship in 1937 to being a third baseman in the Cardinals' system in 1938.

Atlanta Falcons all-pro defensive back Brian Jordan gave up football to become a star outfielder for the St. Louis Cardinals and Atlanta Braves. Running back Bo Jackson hit some of the longest home runs the Southern League has ever witnessed during his time with the Memphis Chicks. Jackson went on to become an all-star in football and baseball before a hip injury ended his career. John Elway, who led the Denver Broncos to the Super Bowl title in 1998, played a year for the Yankees at rookie league Oneonta, New York, batting .318 before switching to football full time.

Author Zane Grey was a pitcher and outfielder until his Western novels became bestsellers. Former New York governor Mario Cuomo played in the Pirates system in the early 1950s. Cowboy movie star Gene Autry played for the Tulsa Oilers. Country singers Jim Reeves and Charley Pride also gave baseball a try. Actor Kurt Russell batted .313 in three seasons in the Northwest and Texas leagues, and Chuck Connors, who played "The Rifleman" on TV during the 1960s, worked his way through the minors and made it to the big leagues for the Dodgers and Cubs.

Many of these stars would have traded their successes elsewhere for long careers in the major leagues.

*Joe Hauser was the first player to hit more than 60 home
runs twice. The first baseman hit 63 for Baltimore in
the International League in 1930 and 69 for Minneapolis
in the American Association in 1933.*

HOME RUN KINGS
OF THE MINORS

Year	Player	Team (Class)	HRs
1954	Joe Bauman	Roswell (C)	72
1933	Joe Hauser	Minneapolis (AAA)	69
1948	Bob Crues	Amarillo (C)	69
1956	Dick Stuart	Lincoln (A)	66
1954	Bob Lennon	Nashville (AA)	64
1930	Joe Hauser	Baltimore (AAA)	63
1926	Moose Clabaugh	Tyler (D)	62
1956	Ken Guatier	Shreveport (AA)	62

Chiefs

Peoria Chiefs Alumni

7

WHERE DREAMS LIVE AND DIE

"When you come to this country the first time, you don't know anything. We always had to go with somebody who spoke English."
—*Chicago Cubs slugger Sammy Sosa*

Minor league players and umpires are far removed from the spoils of major league life. First-class airplane travel, fancy hotels, expensive clothes, and jam-packed stadiums are distant dreams. Six-hour trips on buses without air-conditioning often end at cheap motels without enough hot water. Players usually live in tiny apartments with two or three teammates. Many times they don't have cars. Slugger Cecil Fielder recalled how he and two roommates at Kinston of the Carolina League needed help from a neighbor just to get to the park. "He'd come by at four o'clock every day in his pickup truck and honk the horn, and we'd jump on the back of the truck and he'd take us to the game," Fielder said. "Then, he'd come and get us an hour after the game."

Once players get to the park, being a professional doesn't necessarily mean having the very best. Many minor league stadiums are old and

Fans of the Peoria, Illinois, Chiefs had a chance to see three future stars play in 1985: from left, Greg Maddux, Rafael Palmeiro, and Mark Grace.

have terrible playing surfaces. An infielder will often take a rake out to his position and smooth out the rough spots himself. Players may have to join a gym at their own expense to work out on weights. Each minor league team usually has just two coaches, although the major league team will send out roving batting and pitching coaches for special sessions.

The players adjust to the conditions because they all have the same goal—becoming a big leaguer. But there is nothing that can prepare them for the difficulties off the field, especially with money. With the exception of the top players, who get signing bonuses in the millions, minor leaguers make between $700 and $1,500 a month during the season. In some of the bigger cities that amount will not cover their rent. For the players who are married, the wives may have to hold a job. Cable TV is a luxury. Sometimes having a bed is one, too.

"I was renting an apartment with John Bryant when we played with Charleston, South Carolina, in the South Atlantic League," said Yankees pitcher David Cone. "We had no furniture and we slept on our clothes. We'd ball up clothes to use as a pillow. One day our neighbors threw out a love seat—an old and infested love seat. We scrambled to go out and get it and Lysol it down, and we took turns sleeping on it."

"My first apartment was a hotel room," said Jeff Manto, who spent more than 10 years bouncing around the minors. "I roomed with Willie Frazier. The first guy to wake up took a Styrofoam cooler down the hall to fill it with ice to put on the milk and orange juice. That's what we had. We figured it out that a ballplayer in the

---

Bet You Didn't Know ...

In 1872, a game between two semipro teams in Kansas had become so contested that a riot left many players and fans injured. When the two teams met again a few weeks later, legendary gunfighter Wild Bill Hickock was hired to umpire the game, wearing his six-guns. Not one incident occurred during the game, and as a reward for a job well done, Wild Bill was given a new carriage and two white horses.

low minors is really below the poverty line. People don't realize that."

"The thing about the minors," added Doc Gooden, "is no one—and I mean no one—has any money and a lot of times you have to get your food and hide it because players will mooch off of you. Especially when you've got a pizza. There's always someone trying to get a couple of slices. We had this guy at Lynchburg named Larry McNutt. He'd go by everybody's room and say, 'What've you got to eat in there? What've you got? Got anything to eat?' Gee, he was saving a lot of money because he was eating off everyone else."

Another major league journeyman, Gary Varsho, also spent a lot of time going between the majors and minors. Money was really tight for him and his wife at the beginning of his career.

It's a long way from ballparks like this one in Pikeville, Kentucky, to Yankee Stadium. And for many players starting out, tiny ballparks, cold showers, and long bus rides were a big comedown from the college facilities they were used to.

"I was at double-A and we couldn't afford to carry insurance," Varsho said. "We were just married and one day we're outside playing catch when I hit her with a throw and split her nose wide open. With no insurance, we couldn't afford to go to the hospital."

Foreign players face even more obstacles. When Juan Gonzalez first came to the United States from his native Puerto Rico, he was just 16 years old, had never been away from home, and didn't speak English. Not only was he homesick, he was terrified. "Oh, we were scared to go anywhere," Gonzalez recalled. "We were afraid to even go out and eat."

"It was horrible," said Chicago Cubs slugger Sammy Sosa, a native of the Dominican Republic and Gonzalez's teammate at rookie ball Sarasota in 1986. "When you come to this country the first time, you don't know anything. It was hard for me. It was hard for all of us. You go into McDonald's and you don't know how to order what you want to eat. We always had to go out with somebody who spoke English. We didn't want to go alone because we didn't want to get into trouble—you know, people misunderstanding us. We didn't know how to say anything."

"When you're 16 or 17 and you've never been away from home and then you start to struggle a little bit on and off the field . . . well, I'm not sure people sometimes understand," added Texas Rangers batting coach Rudy Jaramillo.

One element of the minors the foreign players can relate to is racism. While relations are better than they were in the 1960s, players occasionally hear taunts, heckles, and slurs. When Hall of Famer Reggie Jackson was playing for the Oakland A's team in Birmingham, Alabama, in

1967, Jackson was the only black on the team. He couldn't go out to eat with the other players. He couldn't find a place to live.

"[White teammates] Joe Rudi and Dave Duncan let me spend a few nights on their couch," Jackson said. "Then, their apartment manager tried to throw them out because I was staying with them. They said, 'If he goes, we go.' I've never forgotten Duncan and Rudi for it."

The conditions in the minors would make almost any person think of quitting or falling into bad habits. "The only way around it," said San Diego Padres outfielder Tony Gwynn, "is to get locked in and stay focused on the game. My last year in the minors I was in triple-A Hawaii. Now, a lot of guys had a hard time adjusting to that great weather and those beaches. But I was lucky. I never was a beach person, so it didn't distract me."

Catcher Mark Parent, who spent parts of 12 years in the minors, said, "I got married in 1981 and that kept me focused for trying to provide for my family. All the other stuff with the travel, the lousy pay, and the time away from home and my family was all done for a goal—to reach the major leagues. I thought about quitting lots of times and my wife would talk me out of it. Besides, I'm not the quitting type. But it can sure get discouraging and at some point you start to think, 'Hey, maybe this wasn't meant to be.' "

For players such as Mark Parent, baseball is an addiction they can never overcome. They cling to their dream of the big leagues and no amount of time and failure in the minors can keep them from hoping. Sometimes it pays off.

Pitcher Tim Fortugno, who spent parts of three seasons in the majors and 13 in the minors, was 28 years old and had never played above

MINOR LEAGUE MOMENTS

The Longest Game

On April 18, 1981, Rochester and Pawtucket began the longest game in baseball history. Tied 2–2 after 32 innings, the game was suspended at 4 AM on Easter morning. The game was finished on June 23, Pawtucket winning, 3–2, in the 33rd inning. The game lasted eight hours, seven minutes; 156 baseballs were used.

The minor leagues are merciless in sifting out even the most highly touted prospects if they don't produce. In 1989, Pete Rose Jr. broke in with the Erie Orioles of the Class A New York–Penn League. He proved to be no threat to his father's record of 4,256 career hits.

class AA when one of his younger teammates came up to him and said, "Timmy, my dad says you've got to live with the reality that you're a career minor leaguer."

Fortugno said, "What's your dad got to do with it?"

"Well, he says it's because you're 28 years old, you're playing double-A ball and you're not 19, 20, or 21 years old. You're not going to make it."

Fortugno looked in a mirror that day and began to wonder about himself. Maybe it was time to move on. "You never know what's inside your heart," he said, even more determined than ever. The next season he was called up to the California Angels.

Utility player Rich Amaral spent 10 years in the minors, New York Mets pitcher Rick Reed 11 years, and Tampa Bay Devil Rays second baseman Aaron Ledesma eight years before they stuck with a big league team. "Was it worth it?" Amaral said. "You bet."

Pete Rose Jr. was 27 and had played for four organizations in nine years. Then, in the last month of the 1997 season, the Cincinnati Reds, his hometown team and the team for which his famous father had played most of his career, gave him his first chance in the big leagues. Later, Pete Jr. recalled that when he arrived at Riverfront Stadium for the first time as a player, he walked onto the field and "I kind of just looked around and dreamt a little bit."

He started at third base that day against the Kansas City Royals and received a huge ovation from the 31,920 fans, who included his father. When Pete Jr. took the field in the first inning, he reached down and wrote "H.K. 4256" in the dirt behind third base, signifying "Hit King" and his dad's record number of hits in the majors. He used one of his dad's old bats that day and got a single in three trips to the plate. "Today was everything and more," Pete Jr. said. "'Nine years of bus rides, bad food, bad hotels and bad fans—it was all worth it."

By the start of the 1998 season, Pete Jr. was back in the minors. Before the year was over, he had been released twice, never again making the majors. As he sat at home waiting for another team to give him a chance, he was left holding a scrapbook of baseball memories. Most of them were good, some of them bad, but all of them were a priceless experience.

"Sometimes," said manager Jim Leyland of the Colorado Rockies, "I think it would be easier and more fun to just go back to the minors. If it wasn't for the money, I probably would."

MINOR LEAGUE RECORDS

SINGLE SEASON

BATTING

Average
.462   Gary Redus, Billings, 1978

Runs
202   Tony Lazerri, Salt Lake City, 1925

Hits
325   Paul Strand, Salt Lake City, 1923

Doubles
100   Lyman Lamb, Tulsa, 1924

Triples
32   Jack Cross, London, 1925

Home Runs
72   Joe Bauman, Roswell, 1954

Runs Batted In
254   Bob Crues, Amarillo, 1948

Stolen Bases
145   Vince Coleman, Macon, 1983

PITCHING

Wins
39   Doc Newton, Los Angeles, 1904
      Harry Vickers, Seattle, 1906

Strikeouts
456   Bill Kennedy, 1946
       Rocky Mount, 1946

CAREER

BATTING

Average
.370   Ike Boone

Batting Titles
6   Smead Jolley

Hits
3,617   Spencer Harris

Home Runs
484   Hector Espino

Home Run Titles
8   Ken Guettler

Runs Batted In
1,857   Nick Cullop

100-RBI Seasons
12   Buzz Arlett

Stolen Bases
948   George Hogriever

Consecutive Games Played
1,166   Orlando Camarero

PITCHING

Wins
383   Bill Thomas

Games
1,015   Bill Thomas

Strikeouts
3,175   George Brunet

20-Win Seasons
9   Spider Baum

TOP PLAYERS IN
MINOR LEAGUE HISTORY

In 1984, the Society for American Baseball Research surveyed its membership to pick the all-time best minor league players. The 15 players selected:

BUZZ ARLETT, outfielder-pitcher
After winning 29 games as a pitcher in 1920, Arlett switched to the outfield and became a power threat from both sides of the plate. Twice he hit four home runs in a game, and is second with 432 career homers.

IKE BOONE, outfielder
Likely the best pure hitter in minor league history, Boone batted a record .370 over 17 seasons. His 323 hits for the San Francisco Missions in 1929 is the second-highest in minors history.

BUNNY BRIEF, outfielder–first baseman
The American Association career leader in hits, runs, doubles, homers, and RBI, he was an eight-time home run champion. He slugged 340 homers and batted .331 in 18 seasons.

BUSTER CHATHAM, shortstop
A terrific defensive player who stole 312 bases and batted .290 over 22 seasons, he once reached base 15 consecutive times on 11 hits and four walks.

NICK CULLOP, outfielder
A prolific run producer who is the career leader with 1,857 RBI.

HECTOR ESPINO, first base
Playing 24 years in the Mexican League rather than signing with a major league team, he won five batting titles and holds the minor league record with 484 home runs.

OX ECKHARDT, outfielder
An incredible hitter who had 315 hits for the Missions in 1933, when he batted .414, Eckhardt batted .367 for his 13-year career.

TONY FREITAS, pitcher
The top lefthander in the minors with 342 victories, Freitas holds the record with nine 20-win seasons. He posted a 3.11 ERA in 25 seasons.

SPENCER HARRIS, outfielder–first baseman
Harris holds minor league records in runs, hits, doubles, and total bases. In 27 seasons, he had 3,617 hits.

JOE HAUSER, first baseman–outfielder
A powerful lefthander who slugged 399 career homers, "Unser Choe" is the only player to hit more than 60 homers twice—63 with Baltimore in 1930 and 69 with Minneapolis in 1933.

SMEAD JOLLEY, outfielder
Jolley hit 334 homers and won a record six batting titles in 19 seasons.

OYSTER JOE MARTINA, pitcher
Martina won 349 games in 21 years, including seven years with 20 or more victories.

JIGGER STATZ, outfielder
Statz played his entire 18-year career in higher classifications. He won three Pacific Coast League batting titles and finished with 3,356 hits.

PERRY WERDEN, first baseman–outfielder
The top slugger of the 19th century, Werden hit 45 homers for Minneapolis in 1895 at a time when entire teams didn't hit 45 homers in a season. He batted .341 in 24 seasons.

FURTHER READING

Blahnik, Judith and Phillip S. Schulz. *Mud Hens and Mavericks: A Composite History, Information and Team Directory of the Minor Leagues.* New York: Viking Studio Books, 1995.

Chadwick, Bruce. *Baseball's Hometown Teams: The Story of the Minor Leagues.* New York: Abbeville Press, 1994.

Johnson, Lloyd and Miles Wolff. *The Encyclopedia of Minor League Baseball.* Durham, N.C.: Baseball America, 1997.

Kahn, Roger. *Good Enough to Dream.* New York: Doubleday, 1985.

Mayer, Ron. *The 1937 Newark Bears.* New York: Wise & Co., 1982.

Obojski, Robert. *Bush League.* New York: Macmillan, 1975.

Sullivan, Neil J. *The Minors.* New York: St. Martin's Press, 1990.

INDEX

PICTURE CREDITS
Associated Press/Wide World Photos: pp. 33, 36, 40, 42, 44, 47, 49, 58; Courtesy of Butte Copper Kings: p. 26; Courtesy of Durham Bulls: p. 8; Courtesy of Frederick Keys: p. 11; Courtesy of Knoxville Smokies: p. 25; Courtesy of Lubbock Crickets: p. 39; Courtesy of Norman Macht: pp. 2, 6, 12, 20, 22, 24, 51, 55; Courtesy of Peoria Chiefs: p. 52; Courtesy of Richmond Braves: p. 34; Courtesy of Trenton Thunder: pp. 19, 27; David Durochik: p. 30; National Baseball Hall of Fame: pp. 10, 16, 35; Sandquist Collection, Courtesy of the Bisbee Mining and Historical Museum: p. 15; University Microfilms, Inc.: p. 28

DENNIS R. TUTTLE, a native of Walnut Cove, North Carolina, began his sportswriting career at age 17 at his hometown paper, the *Winston-Salem Journal*, in 1977. He has also been a writer and editor at the *Cincinnati Enquirer, Austin American-Statesman, Knoxville Journal,* and *Washington Times*. He is a two-time winner of an Associated Press Sports Editor's Award for sportswriting excellence. His work has appeared in *The Sporting News, USA Today Baseball Weekly, Baseball America, Inside Sports, Washingtonian, Sport,* and *Tuff Stuff* magazines. He authored *Juan Gonzalez, Albert Belle,* the *Composite Guide to Football,* and the *Composite Guide to Basketball* for Chelsea House. He resides in Cheverly, Maryland.

EARL WEAVER is the winningest manager in the Baltimore Orioles' history by a wide margin. He compiled 1,480 victories in his 17 years at the helm. After managing eight different minor league teams, he was given the chance to lead the Orioles in 1968. Under his leadership the Orioles finished lower than second place in the American League East only four times in 17 years. One of only 12 managers in big league history to have managed in four or more World Series, Earl was named Manager of the Year in 1979. The popular Weaver had his number, 5, retired in 1982, joining Brooks Robinson, Frank Robinson, and Jim Palmer, whose numbers were retired previously. Earl Weaver continues his association with the professional baseball scene by writing, broadcasting, and coaching.